Stan Went Fishing

12-16-17

Find yourself in these sweet little stories.

Nancy Dorrier

Paul Fetters

Stories **Nancy Dorrier**
Photography **Paul Fetters**

STORIES AND IMAGES OF WAKING UP

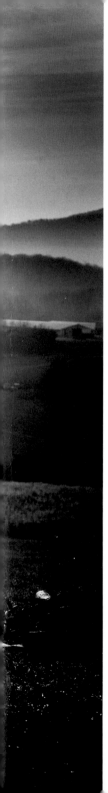

Write Today

Unencumbered of clothes,
CDs, books, shoes, papers —
even food in the cupboard,
files in the computer.

Make a long list of items,
and how many can I take off?

In a real emergency,
most all would come off,
never to get back on.

Get my tooth fixed.
Get my hearing checked.
Send out the boys' March
schedule for guitar.

A writer is not an emergency,
and she will never happen with
all the odds and ends of doing.

Get fresh flowers.
Send a birthday card.
Have Palmer for dinner.
Clean out the clothes in the attic.
And the Christmas decorations.
Write Eric a thank you.
Edit the client plan.

Then at the bottom,
Go work out.

Write today.

What Must You Think?

"Oh, deep in my heart, I do believe we shall overcome some day."

The anthem of a Civil Rights movement, sung again at Clementa Pinckney's funeral, the song started off by President Obama. He and his wife, Michelle, ache and know what that hymn means, down to their gut, for themselves and for their two beautiful black girls.

I know barely, being white, and growing up so privileged that I didn't even notice it. I took it for granted. I take it for granted.

I hardly see anything for my self-concern. Self-concern that blinds me.

Including the thought that, well, I am not *that* self-concerned.

And what must you think?

Columbia Is

isintegrates on Reentry,

Looking for God in the Newspaper

The Lord is my shepherd,
I shall not want.
So with the Lord,
I don't really want anything.

God comes before iPhones and
computers and nice new jewelry.

That is what falling down and
worshipping God means.
Finding solace in God,
in the new painting I got in Santa Fe.
The artist surely was falling down in
front of God, content to paint the light
of Santa Fe over and over and over.

If I was doing that all day, every day,
what would that be like, in a small
studio or outside in a field?

God comes first.
Our yearning for God, actually, first.

Ever-present.
Looking for God in an object,
in someone's eyes,
in a text,
even in the newspaper.
Looking for God
in the conflict in Syria.

Looking in the paper for something
that shows the human spirit at work.

The F-Word

We went outside to cool off and look up at the moon.

Julia was a little homesick, plus, I think she was tired of the banter back and forth in New Delhi accents, nobody really listening to anybody.

She was missing her mother, and most likely her friends.

Yet, she adores her brother and cousins who play and fight and know the F-word and take her to a different world of uproarious laughter and teasing. Isn't that what growth and learning is?

Not just the discomfort of Math and Science, French and Spanish, and learning to play a guitar, but also the discomfort of learning over and over again to be friends with people who think and play and talk differently.

Each time, a little better at navigating and exploring the world.

Meanwhile, she asks in a high-pitched, singsong accent, "Vat's the meening of meening and does it exeest?"

Never said that in her Southern accent.
Never even had it to say.

What Do I Think About It?

Which email?
When?
About what?

Oh that.
Yes, I saw it.

What do I think about it?

That item isn't on my schedule
to deal with, *ever*.
I have my work on my calendar,
and even when I plan to do errands.

Nowhere, anywhere, is there on
my calendar, check email and
answer it, leave the sender informed
with an answer and empowered
by my thoughtful response.

I look for time to pay bills and
do expense reports.
Time to call my friend,
study my Spanish,
and learn to play the ukulele.

Time for anything but answering
your email asking what do I think.

At least the TV hasn't gotten my soul.

And today (yes, after responding
to emails from this morning)
I am getting on Facetime (on the
computer) and listening to Julia
play her guitar.

20	21	22
	New Moon	Winter Begins
27	28	29
	First Quarter	

Last Quarter
15

88 MAXIMA
849-0684

Staring Off

No tension.
No hesitancy.
Just sitting here together looking at the moon.
Rather, lying down looking at the moon —
and a few stars and lightning bugs
looking like stars in the dark trees.
Thrilled at how close.

A little chilly
but not too cold to get up out of bed,
put on some sweatpants and a jacket,
and run out to the field with the quilt
and just lie there.
Her idea.

Mine, to not go,
but couldn't say so.
Couldn't say, Can we just stay in this
warm bed and look at it out the window?
Couldn't say no to such a good idea.

Did say no, some —
enough to kill the buzz.

Needing my own space,
away from the circus of new ideas
and delights
that occur to her.
Since they occurred I must — we must — do them.

What about the good idea of doing nothing?
Sitting on the porch, staring off.

No need to do or be.

I Hope

I'm mostly worried about stepping down into, and then stepping up out of, the boat. And pooping. Not at the same time, more back-to-back worries.

Then Claire told me about having diarrhea in a bucket just before her fox hunts, which really are coyote hunts, in Middle Tennessee. I immediately felt better. I told her how comforting her diarrhea story was. She then said she would help me into and out of the boat, every time.

From now 'til May 21st makes 22 days in April, plus 20 in May.

A mere 42 days. I am clearly counting.

I am in a six-week training program to raft and hike the Grand Canyon. Weight lifting, food plan, walking hills. "Life and death" would be an exaggeration — I hope.

I haven't taken on a project like this since the Marine Corps Marathon, when I was 36.

Different challenge now, approaching 70.

FROM Capt Charles R. Davies O-321323
310th F.A. Bn. APO 79
c/o P.M. New York, N.Y.

Mrs. C. R.

England
May

My Dear, Just

officii

POSTAL
POSTAL SE
79

C. R. Dorrier - O-321323
7. A. Bn. A.P.O. 79
York City

ARMY POSTAL
RMY P

O-321323
ER-CAPT A.P.O. 79
A. Bn.
York City
O-321323
CAPT C. R. Dorrier A.P.O. 79
310th F.A. Bn.
New York City

Mrs. C.
Scot

Thursday 8th Kopp,
1942   are
            hall
    an   to
  communication   old men
  to teach.   the radio
  though. No   see
     you today.   another
       since   remember his
        all. got
              suppose   to
              little   the stag.
                     another wiped
                          Jour
                          Paul
                          lay
  Donnie Jo
  ille
  ginia

Nancy Lee
Has Arrived Safely

Being married.
Someone to laugh with in the middle of the night.
Someone to just sit with.
Someone to check in with and give a little pat.

My parents used to give little pats and two little kisses.

My sister is reading our dad's letters from 1944, written in France during the war, one every day.

This was the time of no devices to check Facebook or text anybody, much less our mom, or watch a movie. Maybe he had a book or a Bible. Definitely, the soldiers had pen and paper and envelopes.

A shoebox of them arrived yesterday from my sister: 1944, the year our mom was pregnant with their fourth child she was sure was a girl. They only had a girl's name ready.

The wartime telegram rule was you could send travel news but not news of a birth.

After my birth, she sent him a telegram:

"Nancy Lee has arrived safely."

Clarity

This new place where neighbors
went to the Church of Christ and
didn't drink. And the Nazarenes,
who didn't drink or dance or wear
makeup. I was a little afraid of them
and their absolute clarity that *they*
were going to heaven.

We were a little band of Presbyterians,
a stone church close enough to walk
to every Sunday morning and on
Wednesdays to church-night suppers
of homemade casseroles, fried
chicken, and pies and cakes.

My mother was in the choir and
my father was an elder.
He gave out mints to keep us quiet.
Sitting next to him, I felt safe.

I didn't know he liked the Nazarenes
and the Church of Christ people.
I didn't know he would give them
a mint too if he was sitting next
to them.

I didn't know what I loved about
him was exactly that.

Deep Dive

This writing, ignorance or pleasure, even genius.

These short stories starting with a line, then going like lightning for five minutes, a deep dive to Old Hickory, Tennessee,

to the room with the scalloped curtains where at night you could see dark through each curve of the scallop where the boogeyman was standing,

and the room where my brother watched *Perry Mason* and ate a whole stack of saltines and a bowl of canned tomatoes and mayonnaise,

and outside the room, my other brother worked on his red motor scooter,

and my sister and I learned how to knit sweaters from our mother, our first project complicated and beautiful.

A deep dive to find out that I love somebody I used to be afraid of,

and that I was safe sitting at the church with my father who would never know William but helped us to be ready for him.

Button

Our financial advisor, Nick, says "you ladies" not
once but several times, and I worry, am I the only
one who hears this in a pejorative, demeaning
way, like someone else hears "you blacks" or
"you people"?

Like Joy, another advisor, says, "If you remember…"
Well no, I don't remember.

Did you really tell me if I don't remember?

Do I have too much sensitivity, irritation,
pent-up-edness?

Unexpressed anger.

To the universe for not helping William,
my seven-year-old grandson, who doesn't talk,
among other things, talk or eat or hold a toy.
Okay for the wheelchair, and okay for the short life.
But let him say "mommy" or even "you ladies."

If that was all that Nick could say, I'd say yes, good,
now let's say "shoelace" or "button."

The Reverend Never Asked

She crawled into bed with her son after he died.

The reverend never asked her to talk.
Only asked would she like a cup of tea or a shawl.

She not talking but saying everything.
"I have gone to heaven with him,
that is where my spirit is."
She knowing her work now is to come back to
earth and be here with the busyness and fun.
Not pulled yet to being there, in the love and
heart song of forever.

While she prepares to move to
four bedrooms, three baths with her
husband and two remaining children,
a pool in the back yard.
There are chores and decisions.

Find a school for the children.
Clean house for the move.
Sort his little tee shirts to make a quilt.

> "I am not flexing my muscles —
>   it would rip my shirt"
> "Most Amazing Brother Ever"
> "Hero"
> "My cape is in the wash"

That could be *her* shirt.

The Promised Land

Thank you, Joyce.

After the funeral of an eight-year-old boy.

Thank you for the lipstick to put a kiss on William's cheek.

Thank you for the joy you brought over to our house every day, all week long.

Thank you for the wine tastings and the bottle of Rutherford House.

Thank you for coming over all made up and beautiful in your red dress and black skin, helping Ray win the bet at the dance.

Thank you for getting Papa to come outside for the hearse ritual.

Thank you for being so faithful and true and beautiful and wise.

Thank you for sitting on the steps for two hours and just being there, nothing to do but a lot to be.

Thank you for carrying your history of celebration of life and death and helping us send William off to the Promised Land.

Lord, have mercy.

Alice-Lyle Says She Just Doesn't Care

She says she just doesn't care, doesn't care about having a house or an apartment, doesn't care how much screen time the kids have, doesn't care about not caring.

Meanwhile, working out, cleaning the house to show it to a buyer, picking up our favorite chicken soup from the Mexican restaurant, fishing the paddle out of the pool, throwing the ball with Mollee.

Sometimes, I feel the same. Then, going for long walks, watching my grandson be Noah in the spring musical and hearing his brother play the bass, I, too, throwing the ball for Mollee, listening to church services on the radio, getting up at 5:45 to write, arranging a trip to the Eastern Shore.

Meanwhile, together we plan the scattering of William's ashes.

Stan Went Fishing

He could not take in what had
happened so he went fishing.

He found himself in the fishing,
again and again swinging his
rod out over the water and letting
his line go.
No one could take in what
had happened.
I never can or could or even want to.
Taking it in trivializes it.
Death is a mystery, as is birth.
The death of a child is
incomprehensible but the birth
is equally so.
It is a mystery.
It is a miracle.

Dad said to Mom, it is okay if you
can't get the Virgin Birth, if you don't
believe it. Birth in and of itself is
a miracle and beautiful to behold
and consider.

Stan could not take in what had
happened so he went fishing.
Went with his dad, another miracle,
now five years sober, swinging their
rods out over the water.

Piebalds for Alice-Lyle

With the sun rising, I wake up
to this birthday: Alice-Lyle 44,
Davis 14. Her first baby, born
on her 30th birthday.

I'm giving her a Freddy Sprock
painting of a mother and baby
lamb, piebalds. Black and white
in the field. It reminds her of her
son, William, gone now. Both she
and Davis miss him.

Alice-Lyle is tenderhearted,
weeping, holding three-month-old
niece Samantha. Grieving
at this family reunion, wishing
they understood that she is
missing what others here call
a burden removed.

I'm giving Davis art supplies.
Nothing related to the screen,
iPhone, X-Box, iPad, and I am
taking him for the massage he
asked for. I give him one each night,
neat, neat, neating, like my
mother did. Pull the covers up
tight, all neat, then press hard
on his back over and over, saying,
"Neat, neat, neat."

Mary at the Beach

We had maps and pencils to track
the long 12-hour trip from Tennessee
to Virginia, to visit family for two
weeks. The second week, all of us
would be at Virginia Beach at the big
Little Cottage on the ocean. Cousins,
aunts, uncles, and Pop, our patriarch
grandfather.

We took Mary to cook for all 25 of us,
three hot meals a day.

She had a room off the kitchen and
little time off. Our parents took turns
planning and shopping for the meals
and overseeing her work.

Occasionally, mid-morning or late
at night, she went to look at the ocean —
certainly not to go on the beach or
touch the water with her black feet.

I loved those summers of walking on
the beach up to the Cavalier Club, to
get a Coke on the rocks for a quarter.

I never thought about Mary not doing
that. I never really thought about
Mary, other than her smile and her
hugs for me.

For me.

Love, N

She called me in tears to tell me
about being pushed around by a
big-dog community leader and
standing up, standing tall, standing
for who she is and what's right.

I emailed her after we talked:
I appreciate your stand for love
and respect.
I appreciate your stand for
organizational life being full, rich,
and productive and honoring the
human spirit.

I am sorry this happened
(*this* being bullying) and
am happy *he* found someone
who is not going to take it.

And who is not accepting of "This is
just the way it is in corporate America."
I love you. I am with you in spirit.
My arms are around you.

Love, N

Before He Was a Father

The alternative resume, like the alternative universe, may be more real than the traditional resume of education and job experience.

I first wrote an alternative resume for my son, Thomas, years ago, before he was a father, that now being one of his biggest talents.

Expert in dog training, especially Chesapeake Bay retriever named Luke Skywalker.

Imitator of Billy Bob Thornton in Sling Blade.

Dance teacher, taught dancing to a boy from India at the School for Math and Science, explaining, "Yes, you do have to touch the girl."

Clotheshorse from the inside: no lumps, no chafing, no scratching, no yucky feeling.

Ukulele player, knows all the words to Lyle Lovett songs and sings a made-up version of "I Love Everybody, Especially You."

Recycle expert, crushes beer cans and plastic bottles, sorts, and hauls to the recycle center.

Quilter, makes quilts on his grandmother's miniature Singer sewing machine.

Advice giver, all sorts.

Lover of everything, especially you.

Not Falling Down

I worked on the front hill in the garden yesterday. I noticed every step before I took it. A new practice: to see a step before I take it rather than when I take it or not see it at all. Fall prevention, a mindfulness practice.

The Buddhist teacher offers walking meditation, slow walking around the yard, all in silence.

What makes the falling?
Being in the past, ruminating?
Or in the future, worrying?

Stepping when you step, would you ever fall?

Or is there just no defense,
no prevention?

Falling, now my fear.
No longer the boogeyman.
No longer money.
No longer love lost.

Falling.
Well that, and losing my mind.

The Problem

Once and yet again, I am wrought up by the ladies and girls thing.

Jim refers to us as "you ladies" and Bobby sometimes refers to "the girls."

And once and yet again, I feel myself not known, resigned, too sensitive, and irritable, and if you have to explain it, what is the point?

One time Chief Whitehorse said exactly that to me. He complained that the setup and some of the points in the course I was leading were offensive, assuming a white person's point of view.

So I said, "Tell me more about that," really wanting to know, and he thought I did.

"Tell me more, tell me the exact offense."

He said, "If I have to explain it, that is the problem."

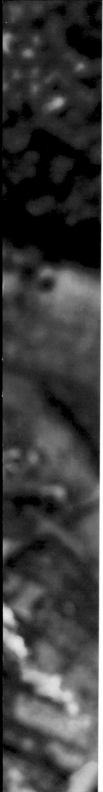

Bless You, Sister

I listened to the radio sermon as
usual, this time on headphones
while I weeded the garden, taking
them off to say good morning to a
churchgoer walking from the bus
at Park Road on his way to Kingdom
Hall of Jehovah's Witnesses.

Later, I took a long walk, collecting
sticks from yards, and picking up a
discarded bag of dog poop thrown
into one yard. I dropped the sticks
next to the curb. A suited gentleman
getting out of his car asks, "Where is
your dog?" I grinned and said, "Can't
you see him, my sweet invisible dog?"

Then I told him that I regularly
collected sticks and trash on my
walks, and today a first — a tossed-
into-someone's-yard bag of dog poop.
He said, tucking his Bible under
his arm, "Give it to me, I will take
it to the garbage."

I gave it to him and he said,
"Bless you, sister."

At 12, a 6

His mind was in swirls the last time I was with him, upset that, at 12, his sister got an iPhone 6. When he was 12, he didn't have a phone at all.

Now they both have iPhones, he a 5 and she a 6, and a phone has become more a small computer than a phone.

A camera, a texting device, an encyclopedia, and a book of maps.

He felt she was favored because she got one.

And I was the culprit, the bad granny again.

He called last night to apologize for being so mad at me, for saying, "I don't know," when I asked if he would ever forgive me for getting his sister at age 12 an iPhone 6.

It is the 6.
And it is that she is 12.

Odd Times in Odd Places

Finding myself in the ice cream store behind the man who stood on one foot and another, selecting what size and flavor coffee he wanted to go with his donut.

I watched myself enjoy his slow decision, and even the clerk's delight and pleasure in helping him.

An odd place because lately I have not been in ice cream stores, not eating dairy and sugar.

But tonight after a long week I went for a pistachio and almond cone, after spending the day with Lucy, finding out about her cancer.

In spite of joining with her on her macrobiotic and super-healthy diet, I said okay to myself.

Tomorrow is a new day.

But then tomorrow, the following day will be a new day.

Can't I get ice cream, as solace for my soul?

Singing at 88th Street

She wanted me to have my own
key to her apartment on West 88th,
so I could let myself in when she
wasn't there.

Her cat, Shiva, roams her 9th floor
apartment and greets me, looking
at me sideways.

She has *no* extra stuff in her apartment,
no piles of papers, few books, just a
piano and recording equipment.

She has a bed in the living room, no
other furniture, a few floor pillows.

Another room with just an overstuffed
chair, her reading room.
And a small kitchen with a place to eat,
open shelves for her pantry of jars with
nuts and seeds and tea.

She is a musician and teacher at
Columbia and sings. When I am there,
I sing with her. We look at each other
and smile. We look at each other like
we have a secret. We do.

Ham Sandwiches and Tea

The scope of your mind
will open enormously, the
meditation book said.

Open enormously, and
you won't know yourself,
you won't know anything you know now,
because you will be in a new land,
a new world
of thinking.

2 plus 2 actually equals 5.

You have tried for years to think that
and understand that
and get that.
Yet you couldn't get it.
It kept being the same wrong answer,
then all of a sudden you saw it,
became it.

And then took your tea and
your ham sandwiches
to the homeless shelter,
and sat and talked.

Finally making sense to you that
this is a place you belong.

Prison and Grace

I don't know what it is like to be in prison,
in recovery, happy that my sentence has been
reduced to two years from four, asking the judge
to move me to a prison that has education
programs. A place to write and work to do.

He just sent his piles of letters to his mother
to save for him, and also my stories. She said
he saved them all.

He is writing a book about the 12 steps, about
serious, no kidding recovery from heroin,
cocaine, marijuana, and from the notion that
you and only you have a higher consciousness
and really see the world for what it is.

Recovery from the false reality of drugged
wisdom, which kept him from doing anything
else but that and, ultimately, got him in prison.

I, recovering every day – and hopefully you, too –
from knowing everything.

Grace.

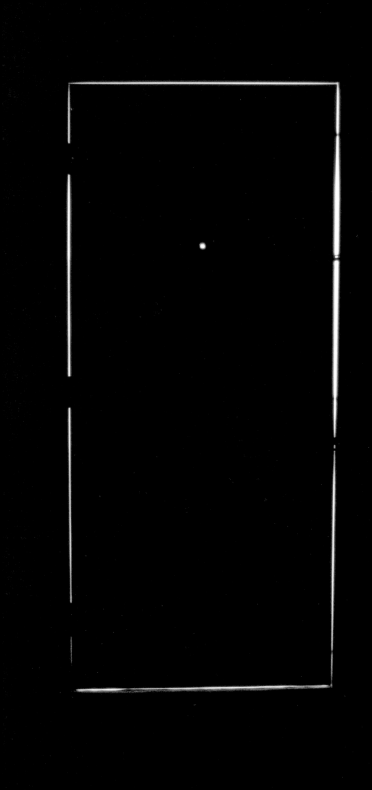

Slivers of Light

Lately I've been paying a good deal of attention to light.

I discovered it in the shadows the mountains made in Santa Fe.

I discovered Georgia O'Keefe. It was *her* light. She couldn't get enough of it. Neither could I.

I bought a painting of that light at the Medicine Man Gallery. Now it hangs on my wall.

Paul loves my little stories, thinks they are beautiful. They open up a new world of seeing and sensing, he says.

Little victories
after an embarrassment,
or nervous laughter
bringing relief to conflict.

My slivers of light, providing special-delivery relief to those in need.

Some days they pour out in these early morning writes or later in the day, calling out, "Write about me, write about that time."

The Muslim family picnicking, an all-American family next to the volleyball court newly filled with sand, grown men kicking the ball back to the girls playing soccer on fields side by side.

Ever-Present

The first thing was a cup of water. Though thirsty, he drank it slowly. Slowly and thoughtfully before he spoke.

Wisdom beyond his years, delight of a child.

Happy to be with me and my offer of water. He, 24, hard at work in the yard, with me, 70, occasionally joining him. Pulling up vinca, finding old pool toys, a plastic shovel, clippers laid down years ago and now found.

Pieces of clay pots, a coffee cup, a rope.

He said, "This grass is tough." A life of its own, tough and strong, ever-present and slow to leave.

He pulled it all, put piles of it next to the street for the city to collect and take out to its place near the airport, to grind up and make into mulch and sell.

We will go get some of it tomorrow to top the garden.

I Grew Up Presbyterian

I grew up Presbyterian, not Catholic.
How you grow up is the right way.
Never mind that Annie Lamott calls
Presbyterians "God's cold people."

Humility sometimes is in short supply
when I think I know something: that it
is wrong not to be offered communion,
and for women not to be allowed to
be priests, and birth control and
homosexual unions, and the wine is
the blood.

I said before the trip that I would love
every ounce of Catholicism, just like
I do when my Catholic chiropractor tells
me stories of church mission work, and
just like I did at my sweet uncle's funeral.

I went to Rome. I walked up the aisle
in the chapel to *not* receive communion.
I walked with my arms folded across my
chest and received a beautiful and holy
blessing from the priest.

Haiku

Lately, I have been reading haiku at the beginning of our company calls.

I had a stack of haiku books on my wrapping table before Christmas. Grandson from a wise old universe, nine-year-old Alexander, picked one up and started reading it to me.

"So simple," he said. "A big meaning in so few words."

So I gave him one of the books, and he read to us at Christmas dinner.

This book was his favorite gift, after his potato shooter and remote-control car.

The shooter and the car, they are *his*. *His* turn. The language of *your* turn is not yet.

The haiku book, he's eager to share; it belongs to all of us.

When the shooter and car are long gone, haiku will still be there.

by the tree
he reached for the toy
his book tucked under his arm

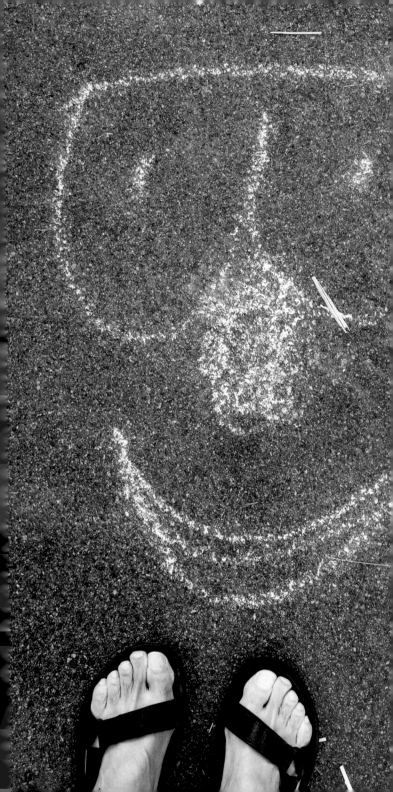

A Friendly Flirt

Waiting there, the man at the vegetable and fruit stand on Highway 17 South — peaches, tomatoes, corn, okra, cucumbers, onions, green beans — waiting to say, "My, you are a tall drink of water."

A friendly flirt.

Sometimes from a stranger in the elevator. Or from me, to the security man at the desk. "You clean up good, looking so handsome in your suit." And he grins and says, "Thank you, ma'am," appropriately. Not, "Well, would you like to come home with me?"

I'm always on the verge of falling in love and sliding all around in the conversation. "Good morning, I am delighted with your countenance," I told Gary, before leading our client summer retreat together.

Enjoying a good friendly flirt when I can.

It Will Be Bumpy

The boss ended her micromanagement, causing chaos, breakdown, and miscommunication. Apologizing for having made a decision without discussing it, and then her team telling her how often she does that and how disruptive it is, and then later feeling bad about it and apologizing.

I told them, "It will be a mess here, it will be bumpy as she moves to her list of Big Ideas and as you move to independent responsibility, a flat organizational chart, away from asking her so many questions."

She named the list My Vision. Hearing her read from the list, a team member said, "Wow, I love that you are doing this."

She is looking at it every day while in meetings, on phone calls, while reading emails. It is taped above her computer.

Asking herself, is this on the list? My Vision.

I Believe In **Red Lion**

WARNING
Protected by
ALARM SERVICE
& Maintenance Co., Inc.
(717) 225-4964

WIN Your Very Own
Memorable Moment
at the 2002 World Series!

Use your MasterCard card between
July 9th and September 20th, 2002,
and automatically be entered for a chance to win.

One Grand Prize:
A Trip for 10 to a World Series® Game

DISCOVER NOVUS

VISA

MasterCard

ATM/DEBIT CARDS & PIN
PREFERRED HERE

STAR

Laudato Si

Reading the Pope's Encyclical,
Laudato Si, I study my lack of awareness
again, this time for indigenous people
and going-extinct-soon plants and
animals and how they are affected by
my thoughtlessness and consumption.

Soaking in the big tub in the mountains,
deep back in Anderson Cove, I hear
Mervil and my fourteen-year-old
grandson, Phillip, debating. The topic
is whether to cook and eat the three big
crawdads he found minding their own
business in the pristine creek.

She doesn't want to and he does.
They call out and ask me to weigh in.

I see both sides.

I see the low impact, except to those
particular crawdads, and say that it is
survival of the fittest, although that
argument is starting to fall apart.

"At least he asked and the kids didn't
just crush them like last year," she says.

In the tub, from the other side of the
curtain, I say,
"And they are tasty, and we are eating
the chicken tonight, aren't we?"

Write This Down

Today, after connecting on many points with a great candidate for our team, I asked: "Glenn, what would take me a long time to find out about you, the good and the bad?"

Without hesitation, he told me about his music career and his deep abiding love for his parents, his love of cooking and holding dinnertime sacred with his family, and the Friday night Seders where everyone comes, even the teenagers.

When I asked, "And the bad?" he said, without hesitation, "I don't write things down. In the moment, I am not thinking of the future moment when I will need the information, and that has gotten me in trouble. I'm also more afraid than I look. I am filled with fear." He said it with a little catch in his throat, afraid as he said it.

I told him that I, too, was afraid. As consultants, we know it's universal; it's not personal, it is everywhere.

And we pretend it is nowhere.

"So write this down," I said to him.

Floundering and Stumbling

Floundering and stumbling between moments of clarity and peace of mind. Floundering and stumbling, I must find my way counting less on certainty and clarity. Because the ways I'm going are rough and muddy and steep, or because I lack the strength to carry on. Mostly the first.

I could do more sit-ups and squats and weight lifting, and get my heart rate to 150 on the elliptical. I could do more strength building for the muddy hills, hope to goodness I will.

But mostly it's that the ways are rough and muddy and steep, and those are the ways I'm looking for, assigned to, and called to.

Go and find the vision of a great leader and find the difficulties in the way, and take them. Take them one by one, each one bigger than the last, but each one easier than the first.

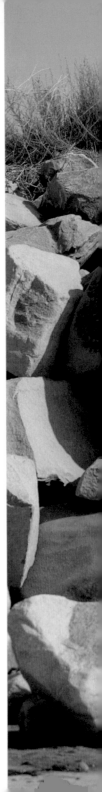

Not the One In Charge

His eyes, his smile, his pat, his hug, say, "I love you," or "I'm sorry," or "I like you." Which he doesn't say directly.

I told my brother that I had brought several bottles of wine to the dinner.

My brother, the incessant hard teaser, sometimes sharp-edged, said, "I'm not in charge."

I asked, "And who is?" And he said, teasing, "Just show up and contribute, don't ask me."
I moved away, duly chastised, and felt ten years old and wrong again.

The next night, when I brought red wine to Stephanie's meatball dinner, my brother and his son circled around the table, looking at the labels, talking about it, and he said, "Should we open it and let it breathe?"

I smiled and patted *him* this time, saying, "Well, I don't know, you're not the one in charge."

He laughed and gave me a pat.

Julia and the One-toothed Man

The man at the convenience store on Highway 521, south of Manning, had one tooth in his mouth. You could see it when he smiled, lower left jaw.

Julia, 11, wanted to hold my hand and suggested we not stop here, that we get back in the car and go somewhere else.

The one-toothed guy and I chatted about the lost flip-flop I found in the parking space next to my car.

I held Julia's hand and said, "The full drink from the Subway in Kershaw has gone through my system, and I need to go to the bathroom here."

We stayed together, side by side, standing in line for the one-toilet bathroom.

On our trip yesterday, it was the man at the BI-LO who bagged our groceries and chatted. Married 51 years, he said she died three years ago of Lou Gehrig's disease.

"Congratulations, and I'm sorry," I said.

Beloved characters abound.

Today, it is the one-toothed man.

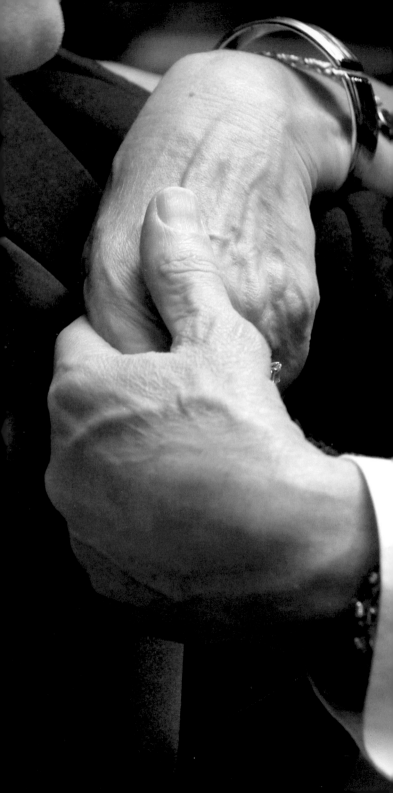

Little Pats

Little pats, the solution until
you stop to consider the nature
of the problem.

The problem of taking down the
Berlin Wall.
The problem of ending apartheid.
The problem of this election.
The problem of these immigrants.

The problem of a relationship.
It should be possible until you
stop to consider it.
Each of us has to hold the other,
versus blame and be impatient.
Or each of us has to blame and
be impatient, then start all over.

Learning that early on,
and now engrained in my cells.
Happy not to have to work it out.

Yet knowing I am missing the
miracle of doing exactly that.

Like my sister has for 50 years,
and my brother for 40,
in sweet relationships.
Sometimes perturbed but
still holding hands and
giving little pats.

Distant Second

At first he didn't know what to do with
the Board of this special private school
he was leading.

He asked, "Isn't that the Board's job anyway?
Knowing what to do?"

I said, "Well, I don't know, is it?"

He was always engaged — now he had
become engaging.

Now, this headmaster is looking more for
advice than money, and the Board is
providing both.

The question for him today:

What is your purpose here?

What about education?

Is it only for the young?

What are people saying yes to, being on
the Board, and yes to, being donors?

What are they looking for, by being around
you and this progressive little school?

This place where teachers look at learning
disabilities as merely part of the wonder
of how we learn.

And coaches use sports primarily as an
experience of play and participation,
with winning a distant second.

Camp Nana

I walk on the path to the beach and
my son, Thomas, rises to assist me
with my folded beach chair and asks,
"Where do you want it?" And I say,
"Right next to you."

"Tell us about Camp Nana," he says.

My annual one-week granny
camp for the grandchildren in
the mountains of North Carolina.

I tell him of conversations, mule rides,
and crawdads. And the hot tub, where
the water circulated every 20 minutes,
fed by the hot springs next to the
French Broad. We shampooed and
body washed twice each and made our
resolutions for the new school year:

> Make new friends, share secrets.
> Speak up more.
> Do my homework — I mean,
> the way it is meant to be done.
> Have better manners,
> be kind to people.
> Thank the teachers.
> Hold the door, don't always go first.

I didn't tell him about letting the
kids ride on top of the Suburban, five
miles per hour down the dirt road.

Rocking, Not Screaming

Watching *Pitch Perfect 2*, about a
competition of college students
singing a cappella.
Before that night I thought it
was about baseball.

I looked over at my daughter
and she pointed to Davis's head
in her lap and smiled.

Each birth blesses a house
and comes straight from God.
Each one owns the universe.
Is the universe.
And then slowly and surely each
one finds out no, that isn't true,
there are other people here you
have to think of.
You can't just scream at the top
of your lungs in church.

Lucy wailed in the doctor's office
after saying, "I think I need to
make a noise." This after sitting
on the exam table, rocking, as
she listened to her doctor give
the pathology report.

Davis, 14.
Lucy, 54.
Both blessed their houses,
and still blessing my life.

I, rocking, not screaming.

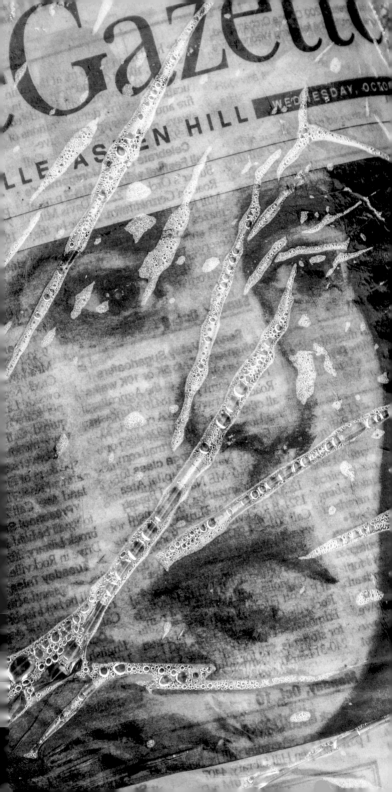

Lucy Has the Cancer

She has the cancer.
Fast-growing cells multiplying.

They removed her uterus. It weighed five pounds.
We went to the lab and saw it, as big as a baby and
twice the size of Julia's new puppy.

What is she going to do with the rest of her life?
Mary Oliver's question: "What are you doing
with your one wild and precious life?"

We talked about the recommended treatment
options, and whether she was she going to take
them or go the alternative route or both.

Will her husband yell at her for not just taking
the doctor's recommendation?
Will I protect her from his yelling?
I kept asking what does she want to do
with her life.

And what does she make of this challenge,
the cancer and Kenny yelling.

I asked her, do you know that yellers are the
scaredest and lovingest of all?

She snuggled under the quilt.

Untouchable

Watching a film about the Dalai
Lama this morning, the part about
the hang-glider tourists spending
more money than an untouchable
spends in a lifetime, the untouchable
looking up in the sky as the tourists
drift overhead at the foot of the
Himalayas.

What adventure will they go on next?
Which will I go on?

Seeking the rewards of travel and
new worlds over the satisfaction of
sitting and drinking tea in the slum.

Being afraid of the squalor but not
afraid of jumping out of a plane.

Being afraid to sit and look into a
stranger's eyes.

Being afraid to go to the party when
I can't hear anyway.

Writing daily to work this out,
finding moments for more love
and less hardheartedness.

Washing the Grapes

I was washing grapes for him.

Happily and naturally.

I learned it from my mother.
It was invisible learning.
I learned it from watching her
take care of my father, and he her.
Looking at the whole of a party.
Seeing when someone's
water glass is empty.
Offering another serving.
Passing the bread on to
the next person, not just saying,
No thank you, and not passing it.
We were taught those basics
when we were six years old.
Don't just serve yourself first.
Serve the other first.
Don't start eating until
we are all served.
Hold the door.
Say, Yes, ma'am, and Yes, sir.
And No, thank you.
I am so glad to be here
and to meet you.
Thank you for inviting me.
Whether we meant it or not.
Though once we said it,
we meant it.

Things I Didn't Know

I think there are things I didn't know about, and then all of a sudden I did. Like now I know about Malaysian Airlines and mudslides, and now I know about Grant Wood, the artist.

But I don't really remember when I found out about him. I don't know when I learned about peanut butter-mayonnaise-and-banana sandwiches. Some things, it seems, I have always known.

I haven't always known about losing love, being in love deeply and profoundly, and then poof, it is gone. I didn't always know that my brother was dead until one moment — then I always knew it.

I don't think you can ever be familiar with that, maybe like you can't ever be familiar with the moon, the full moon, or the weather, the new spring or the intense winter. So we talk about it and exclaim.

I didn't always know Paul, the photographer, then one day I met him, and in a moment we fell in complete appreciation for each other's work, each other's art of expressing the tension of being alive, the foreverness of it, moment by moment, the yearning to be awake and not miss it. We can't find enough ways to say it.

Acknowledgments

We appreciate:

Jane Smith and Doug McVadon for looking at our photographs and listening to our stories on Saturday morning group reading calls.

And Lucy Lustig whose journey and love of life we celebrate with this book.

Participants in the Red Truck Program, for their commitment to expressive writing.

Nancy Chek for her joy of transformation through writing and love of good literature.

Lee Thompson for her whole-hearted encouragement and belief in this book.

Natalie Goldberg, Irene Honeycutt, and Zelda Lockhart, extraordinary writing teachers who open worlds for their students.

Our friends who read and laughed and cried and said, go for it.

Irene Owsley, Rick McCleary, and Hannele Lahti, the "Camera Club."

Mervil Paylor for her artistic vision and the joy she brings to her work (especially on this precious project).

Our family of grandchildren, children, sisters, and brothers who agreed to be our subjects, especially William Eli Hickson — after all, he is why Stan went fishing.

Writing this book has been a true joy, and we want to acknowledge one another for how we listen and appreciate each other's work. Without that, this book would not have happened.

— *Nancy and Paul*